Meet the
Monkeys

Meet the Monkeys

written and illustrated by
Martha Dickson Allen

Prentice-Hall, Inc. Englewood Cliffs, N.J.

Thanks also to N.J. Van _____ ____ _____, ____burg, Virginia, and to Ron Harrison, photographer, San Diego Zoo, San Diego, California. I am especially indebted to Mike Morgan and Linda Mahn of the National Zoo, Washington, D.C., Nellie Johns of the Yerkes Regional Primate Center, Emory University, Atlanta, Georgia, Dr. S.S. Kalter, Director, and Dr. Heberling, of the Southwest Foundation for Research and Education, San Antonio, Texas, and the monkeys of the National Zoo, Washington, D.C. and the Catoctin Mountain Zoological Park, Thurmont, Maryland.

Printed in the United States of America   J

Prentice-Hall International, Inc., London
Prentice-Hall of Australia, Pty. Ltd., North Sydney
Prentice-Hall of Canada, Ltd., Toronto
Prentice-Hall of India Private Ltd., New Delhi
Prentice-Hall of Japan, Inc., Tokyo
Prentice-Hall of Southeast Asia Pte. Ltd., Singapore
Whitehall Books Limited, Wellington, New Zealand

10   9   8   7   6   5   4   3   2   1

Library of Congress Cataloging in Publication Data

Allen, Martha Dickson.
  Meet the monkeys.

  SUMMARY: Describes the behavior, physical appearance, identifying characteristics, and natural habitat of 32 species of monkeys.
    1. Monkeys—Juvenile literature.
  [1. Monkeys—Habits and behavior] I. Title.
  QL737. P9A564   599'.82   78-26211
  ISBN 0-13-574202-1

To Scott and Jason. And to Rick.

Table of Contents

Introduction. 9

PRE-MONKEYS. 13

    The Tarsier. 15
    The Potto 17
    The Sifaka 19
    The Woolly Indri 21

NEW WORLD MONKEYS 25

    The White-Faced Saki 27
    The Capuchin 29
    The Red Howler 31
    The Red Uakari 32
    The Golden Lion Tamarin 34
    The Spider Monkey 37
    Humboldt's Woolly Monkey 39

OLD WORLD MONKEYS 43

The Hamlyn Guenon 45
The Patas Monkey 47
The Black-Crested Mangabey 49
The Gray-Cheeked Mangabey 51
The Doguera Baboon 53
The Hamadryas Baboon 55
The Barbary Ape 57
The Lion-Tailed Macaque 59
The Japanese Macaque 61
The Celebes Black Ape 63
Kirk's Red Colobus 65
The Black and White Colobus 67
The DeBrazza Guenon 68
The Douc Langur 70
The Proboscis Langur 73
The Celanese Gray Langur 75
The Mandrill 77

THE APES 81

The Lar Gibbon 82
The Siamang 85
The Orangutan 87
The Chimpanzee 89
The Mountain Gorilla 91

Bibliography 93

Index 95

INTRODUCTION

Seventy-five million years ago when the dinosaurs were dying, tiny furry animals began scampering about the earth. They ate the dinosaur eggs and soon the giant reptiles disappeared altogether. But these small furry animals survived. Day-sleeping, night-prowling creatures, they were about the size of rats or moles, with popping eyes and hands shaped like ours. For thousands of years they lived in trees and ate insects. Then, as the seas which covered much of the earth began to recede, the world and its inhabitants began to change. These small animals grew, their posture changed, their brains grew larger, and they eventually became our cousins, the Primates.

Primates are mammals, warm-blooded animals with fur on their bodies. They have more advanced brains than other animals, flexible hands and feet usually having five fingers and toes, and their bodies are especially designed for living in trees. There are several forms of Primates: the pre-monkeys, the monkeys, the apes, and man. We, obviously, have come down from the trees.

The study of our monkey and ape relatives is interesting and important. Through it we can gain a better understanding of ourselves, where we came from and how we developed. Learning how primates have adjusted or failed to adjust to their changing environments can be vitally important to the survival of the human race.

Sadly, many primates are disappearing from the earth today. The building of highways, the cutting of timber, and the development of new farmlands are destroying their native forest homes. Wars in Asia and Africa have destroyed the animals as well as their environments. Primates are also hunted—for food, for their skins, for the pet and zoo trade, and for medical research. The number of these animals left as well as the rain forests where many of them live are shrinking at an alarming rate. Several of the monkey species described in this book are in danger of extinction.

There are one-hundred thirty-one different monkey species. In the following pages you will meet thirty-three of the most interesting species alive today.

Pre-Monkeys

PRE-MONKEYS

On the island of Borneo to this very day live animals almost exactly like those furry prehistoric creatures. And throughout the world hundreds of their relatives survive. All of them belong to the Primate group.

These small, furry animals are known as Prosimians. Prosimian is the scientific name given to pre-monkeys or half-monkeys. Prosimians are called pre-monkeys because they are in between the insect-eating animals like lizards, and monkeys who eat plants, leaves, fruit, insects and other animals. Pre-monkeys are nocturnal which means they sleep during the day and are active at night.

For millions of years these pre-monkeys were found all over the world. But today there are only a few left in Africa and Asia. Many Prosimians are so much like the animals of eighty million years ago that scientists are learning how our earliest ancestors lived by studying both fossils and the Prosimians that are still alive today.

THE TARSIER

Size:

   Weight: 3-4 ounces (85-113 grams)

Habitat:

   Borneo, the Philippines, and the Indonesian island of Celebes

Description:

   The Tarsier has enormous eyes, a hairy nose with nostrils facing sideways, and large ears. Its long tail is almost hairless. There are round suction discs at the ends of its fingers and toes and its fur is thick and woolly.

The Tarsier is one of the smallest of all the monkey species. It is about the size of a rat or chipmunk. Its huge eyes are bigger in proportion to its body than those of any other monkey. Scientists consider the Tarsier one of the "oldest" mammals now living on earth because it so closely resembles fossils of animals that lived millions of years ago.

Tarsiers have very long legs and can leap six feet forward and hop four feet high. Muscular pads on the ends of their fingers and toes enable them to cling by suction to smooth surfaces.

Tarsiers can move their heads completely around, 180 degrees, so they often look as though their heads are on backwards. They also can roll their eyes up and down and sideways so only the whites of their eyeballs show and they look very spooky.

These animals have a shrill, bird-like call and are easily excited. If teased, the Tarsier will stand up on its hind legs, clench its fists and spar like a boxer.

THE POTTO

Size:

Height: 14-16 inches (35-41 centimeters) with 2-3 inch (5-7½ centimeter) tail

Habitat:

Nigeria and the Congo

Description:

The Potto has big, round, startling eyes, rounded ears, and thick dark brown fur. Its thumbs and big toes are long but its index fingers and second toes are short.

Since the Potto looks like a little bear it has earned the nicknames honey bear, bush bear, and tree bear. Pottos move very slowly and rarely jump. For this reason the West Africans call this monkey a name which means "softly softly".

African legends tell of Pottos being lazy and say they don't take as many as ten steps in a single day. One legend holds that a Potto never leaves a tree until it has eaten all the fruit and leaves on it, and if the tree is tall, a Potto may die of hunger because it's too lazy to climb down and go to another. But in reality, if Pottos have to, they can move very fast.

Pottos have an unusual physical trait which no other monkeys have. There are horny spines on the backs of their necks which can penetrate their skin. If Pottos are threatened they lower their heads and use these spines as a weapon.

THE SIFAKA

Size:

Height: 18-23 inch (46-58 centimeter) body with tail about the same length
Weight: 13 pounds (6 Kilograms)

Habitat:

Forests of Madagascar, a large island in the Indian Ocean, off the southeastern coast of Africa

Description:

The Sifaka has golden eyes and long, silky white fur with markings in many colors. Its muzzle is short, black and furless and it has long powerful hindlegs for jumping.

Sifakas can jump over thirty feet in one leap and often walk upright rather than on all fours. Tribes on Madagascar believe these monkeys are reincarnated sunworshippers because they like to sun themselves. They lie with arms and legs outstretched and turn their heads lazily from side to side. When their undersides are warmed up, they turn over and sun their backsides.

Sifakas love to touch each other and to cuddle. Newborn babies cling to the fur on their mothers' abdomens and leave only to nurse. Older Sifakas often wrestle playfully. They eat only leaves, fruit, flowers and seeds—no meat or insects. They use their teeth more than their hands while eating and often drop more than half their food on the forest floor.

When Sifakas see humans they act very strangely. They gather around, lick their noses, weave their heads from side to side, and stare. Then they make a noise that sounds like the word "sifaka". Is that our name for them or their name for us?

THE WOOLLY INDRI

Size:

  Height: 30 inches (76 centimeters) tall with a tail only one
  inch (2½ centimeters) long
  Weight: 13 pounds (6 kilograms)

Habitat:

  Volcanic mountains and coastal regions of northeastern
  Madagascar

Description:

  The Woolly Indri has a short, black furless face. Its body is
  covered with thick black and white fur.

"Indri," which means "Look, there it is," is the word natives called to each other when they came upon this monkey sleeping in the forest. Indris make loud wailing noises as they roam the forests at night and their big eyes and furry bodies make them look rather ghostly.

The Indri's thick fur is usually black and white, but some Indris have red on their flanks and heels, which makes them look like they are wearing socks and gloves. Pure white albino Indris with pink eyes also exist.

Indris always sit erect and on the ground they hop along on their hind feet, holding their bodies upright. Perhaps for this reason natives on Madagascar believe the Indris are really people who ran into the woods to hide from enemies and turned into animals.

The natives never hurt them. They believe if you throw a spear at an Indri the animal will catch it and throw it back at you.

The Woolly Indri is in danger of extinction.

New World Monkeys

NEW WORLD MONKEYS

New World Monkeys live in the tropical jungles of Central and South America and in the West Indies. They have broad noses and some have "prehensile" tails. Prehensile means "fifth hand", which describes the way these monkeys use their tails. They can pick up objects with them or wrap their tails around a branch and dangle head downward to pick things up from the ground. The skin on the inside, gripping part of the tail is extremely tough and the tails are slender so they can wrap easily and tightly around a branch.

THE WHITE-FACED SAKI

Size:

  Height: 40 inches (102 centimeters)
  Weight: 3-3½ pounds (11.36-11.6 kilograms)
Habitat:

  The tropical rain forests of Venezuela, Guiana and Brazil
Description:

  The White-Faced Saki has very thick, coarse fur, a bushy tail
  and hairy head. Males have black coats with white faces.
  Females' faces are dark.

The Sakis are sad-looking, shaggy animals. Their long, uneven fur is so thick that rain can't penetrate it. Male Sakis have an elaborate hood of hair which grows from a circle on the back of the neck and hangs down over the forehead.

When a Saki gets mad it stands on its back legs and grinds its teeth. And getting its beard wet makes this monkey madder than anything. So when a Saki wants a drink, instead of bending its face down to the river, it dips its hairy hand in and then licks the water off the fur. This way, its beard and face stay dry.

Sakis like to run along branches on their hind legs with their arms stretched high above their heads and their fingers spread wide apart. Sakis have two thumbs. Their faces turn bright red when they get excited or stay in the sun too long. They are often a comical sight.

THE CAPUCHIN

Size:

    Height: 12-15 inch (30-38 centimeter) body with 24 inch (61 centimeter) tail

    Weight: Males 2½-7 pounds (1.15-3.32 kilograms)

Habitat:

    Rain forests of South America

Description:

    Capuchins have hairless faces with tufts of hair over the eyes or along the side of the head. Their fur is either grayish-brown or patterned with patches of white on the face, throat and chest.

Capuchins are the monkeys which were used by organ grinders and they are the most common species of monkey in captivity today. They were named for the crest of dark hair on their heads which resembles the cape worn by Capuchin monks. This hair looks like it's been brushed in every direction and gives them a comical appearance.

Capuchins are quite intelligent and make gentle and affectionate pets. They are very curious animals and like to take things apart to see how they work. Capuchins learn tricks easily and never forget them. They have been known to paint pictures and scribble. And they like to show off all these talents to gain human attention.

THE RED HOWLER

Size:

  Height: 4 feet (122 centimeters)
  Weight: Males 16-20 pounds (7.2 kilograms). Females 12-18 pounds (5.1 kilograms).
Habitat:

  Central and South America from northern Argentina to Southern Mexico
Description:

  The Red Howler has a thick heavy neck and somewhat hunched appearance. When its mouth is open the rest of its head is practically hidden. These monkeys have black, brown or red fur.

The Red Howler is the largest monkey in South America. Its incredible howl sounds like the roar of a passing train and can be heard for miles. This amazing noise is due to two rounded bony "sound boxes" about two inches deep, which are inside the throat skin between the sides of the lower jaw. The roar begins in the throat and as the rush of air from the lungs sweeps across the openings at the tops of the boxes it becomes much louder. It works much like blowing very hard across the top of an empty bottle.

The male Howlers wake up very early and begin howling while the females bark like terrier dogs. They are warning other groups to stay out of their territory. After this early morning howling the monkeys eat and lie around in their trees.

Howler Monkeys never jump from branch to branch as most other monkeys do. Instead adult monkeys form a bridge between trees with their arms and tails and the babies cross over their bodies to the next tree.

THE RED UAKARI

Size:
   Height: 16-18 inches (41-46 centimeters)
Habitat:
   The rain forests of southwestern Brazil
Description:
   The Red Uakari's body is skinny and covered with shaggy
   hair, except on its head. Large jaw muscles can be seen
   clearly through the bare skin on its long bony face. Its fingers
   and toes are very long, slender and pink. It is the only South
   American monkey with a tail shorter than its body.

The pink-faced Red Uakari is one of the most ghastly-looking of
all monkeys. It is the size of a cat and lives in the highest tree
branches. Some say it never comes down to the ground.

The natives of South America once used poison blow guns to
catch the Uakari. When the monkeys were hit by the darts,
hunters would catch them as they fell from the trees and put a bit
of salt in their mouths to counteract the poison. Adults were eaten
and babies were taken as pets.

The Uakaris are close relatives of the Saki and have the same
sad look. Their faces are pink but turn bright red when they get
excited or spend a lot of time in the sun. Their bodies are covered
with long, shaggy, rust-colored hair, in startling contrast to their
bald heads. The noises they make sound like hysterical laughter.

Uakaris are uneasy on the ground, and are seldom observed in
the wild. They don't like captivity, and have never had babies in a
zoo. But they will invent games for themselves, sliding across the
floor of their cages or turning somersaults backwards.

THE GOLDEN LION TAMARIN

Size:

 Height: 6-10 inches (15-25 centimeters) with a 10-16 inch (25-41 centimeter) tail
 Weight: 9-18 ounces (255-510 grams)

Habitat:

 Forests of southeastern Brazil near Rio de Janeiro

Description:

 The Golden Lion Tamarin has beautiful golden yellow fur, a gray hairless face and blue eyes. Its hands and feet are long and narrow and there is a long silky mane on top of its head.

These little monkeys are the most vividly colored mammals in the world. They live in the lower branches of tall trees in the Brazilian rain forests. High strung, alert, and curious, they chatter like birds as they leap through the trees and feed on insects, fruits, and seeds.

Golden Lion Tamarins are friendly with the other monkey species who live on the branches above them. But when they get angry their hair stands on end; they make faces, jerk their heads from side to side, and scream! They sleep with their tails covering their heads.

Like humans, Tamarins are particular in choosing their mates. Mothers always bear twins and will care for them for only five days. On the sixth day they turn the care of the babies over to the father.

Timber cutting poses a special problem for the survival of this species. Golden Lion Tamarins are unable to live anywhere but in the oldest parts of the forest, making their homes in the holes of rotting trunks and branches. Replanting destroyed forests will not preserve their habitat. There may be as few as a hundred Tamarins left in the wild.

The Golden Lion Tamarin is in danger of extinction.

THE SPIDER MONKEY

<u>Size:</u>

Height: 16-26 inches (41-66 centimeters) with 24-36 inch (61-91 centimeter) tail
Weight: 12-15 pounds (5.5-6.8 kilograms)

<u>Habitat:</u>

Central and South America from Southern Mexico to Uruguay

<u>Description:</u>

The Spider Monkey is slender with skinny arms and a bulging stomach. Its coarse, wiry hair ranges from red to black.

When a Spider Monkey walks along a limb the joints of its legs stick up like a spider's, which is how it got its name. These monkeys are great acrobats and can move fast and gracefully from tree to tree. But they have bad tempers and are jealous and unpredictable.

Spider Monkeys will shake branches, bark, and throw limbs when they see humans. If other monkeys intrude, all the adults will rush to the ends of their branches, bark loudly, shake the branches, and scratch themselves.

When Spider Monkeys get lost they make a whimpering noise like the neigh of a horse. An answering call from another monkey will guide the lost one home.

HUMBOLDT'S WOOLLY MONKEY

Size:

    Height: 16-20 inches (41-50 centimeters) with a tail 22-28 inches (60-71 centimeters) long

    Weight: 7½-20 pounds (3.3-9 kilograms).

Habitat:

    Forests of South America

Description:

    Humboldt's Woolly Monkey is pot-bellied with close woolly fur. Because of its short snout, its flat, black face looks very human. Its fur can be chocolate brown, pure brown, dark gray, or silvery gray.

It has been said that a Woolly Monkey will die if it doesn't get enough love. These monkeys are very gentle and affectionate and make good pets. They are also very clean and can even be toilet-trained.

Baby Woollys are so playful some can't sit still, even for a minute. Woollys laugh and cry, shake their heads and chuckle out loud when playing alone. When they are sad, they cover their eyes with their hands, hang their heads down, and make sobbing noises just like a human.

The Woollys are also chest rubbers. Several times a day they wet their lips with saliva and rub the saliva over a special place or object. Then they push their chest over the wet surface and in this way mark their territory.

The Woolly's body is heavy and covered with thick fur. Its tail is as strong and large as the arm of a human. There are many Woollys in zoos but legend has it that in their natural homes they stay high in the treetops and never come down to the ground.

Old World Monkeys

OLD WORLD MONKEYS

Old World Monkeys live in the tropical and subtropical parts of Asia, from Japan to Thailand, down through Malaysia and into the South Pacific Islands. There is a large population of Old World Monkeys in Africa, reaching from the equator all the way down to the Cape of Good Hope. India and the countries surrounding it, as well as many islands in the Indian Ocean, are also Old World Monkey homes.

Old World Monkeys greatly outnumber New World Monkeys. However, not a single one is able to hang by its tail. Some have practically no tails at all. Old World Monkeys have noses that point downward with nostrils that are very close together. They also have tough, callous pads on their rumps, to make sitting in trees more comfortable.

THE HAMLYN GUENON

<u>Size:</u>

Height: 28-70 inches (71-178 centimeters)

<u>Habitat:</u>

The eastern Congo

<u>Description:</u>

Approximately twenty different species of Guenons exist. They are some of the most colorful monkeys in the world. Some are green with red tails. Some are blue. Some are dark purple. Some have beards. Some have red ears. The Hamlyn is a beautiful silky animal with a white stripe running down its nose and a cap of hair covering its ears.

The Hamlyn looks like an owl. It is very rare and moves in an unusual way. Instead of leaping from tree limb to tree limb Hamlyns crash into the leafy branches, grab hold, and then fling themselves towards the next branch. This method of traveling looks like slapstick comedy but Hamlyns move as fast through the trees as a man does on the ground.

When everything is peaceful Hamlyns keep up a steady conversation of grunts and croaks. But when danger threatens they freeze in the highest branches and stay completely quiet. If confronted by their enemies they make faces, make honking noises and yawn. They don't yawn because they're tired; yawning helps them stay calm.

In the forest, the crowned eagle is the Hamlyns' worst enemy. This eagle swoops down out of the sky and grabs the monkeys from their home in the treetops.

THE PATAS MONKEY

Size:

Height: Males are 3 feet (91 centimeters) long and have a tail almost the same length. Females are 1½ feet (46 centimeters) long with the same size tail.

Weight: Males weigh approximately 25 pounds (11 kilograms). Females weigh 11-15 pounds (5-6/8 kilograms).

Habitat:

The deserts and grasslands of equatorial Africa from Senegal to Ethiopia

Description:

The Patas is a large red monkey built like a greyhound dog with a deep chest, muscular back and long legs for running. Its coat is dark red on top and off-white underneath.

Patas are sometimes called military monkeys because their coat looks like the uniform worn by nineteenth century cavalrymen, and because they move in a military fashion. However, Patas are soldierly in no other way. They never organize and fight their enemies but instead hide from them in the tall grasses or run away at high speeds. And rather than remaining close to each other at night these monkeys sleep far apart so if one is attacked the others will have a good chance of getting away. They are so fast they are called the "Primate cheetahs."

Troops of Patas are always led by a female and there is only one adult male in every troop. The male acts as watchdog and decoy. The other males roam about in bachelor bands.

Patas are very quiet animals and make a chirrup sound when disturbed. But there is one thing Patas will definitely quarrel about. And that is who gets the mushrooms. They eat a variety of foods but mushrooms are their favorites. They love them so much that Patas mothers will steal them from their young.

THE BLACK-CRESTED MANGABEY

<u>Size:</u>

Height: Males are 18-24 inches (46-61 centimeters) long.
Females are a little smaller.

<u>Habitat:</u>

The forests of equatorial Africa from Senegal to Ethiopia

<u>Description:</u>

The Black-Crested Mangabeys have slender bodies, oval
heads and large hands and feet. There are gray whiskers on
their cheeks and long black hairs which stand up in a crest on
the tops of their heads.

Black-Crested Mangabeys live high up in the trees and on the
ground they move rather awkwardly, probably because of their
large hands and feet.

These monkeys are great grimacers and like to show their teeth.
The gray whiskers that fan out from their cheeks and chin make
them look rather funny. And the long black hair that stands up in a
peak on their heads adds to the effect.

The Mangabeys have cheek pouches which they use for storing
raw food when it is first caught. Later when they have more time,
they chew and swallow at their leisure.

THE GRAY-CHEEKED MANGABEY

Habitat:

Equatorial Africa from French Guinea to Uganda

Description:

The Gray-Cheeked Mangabey is a large monkey with crests of hair on its head and feathery tufts fanning out from its cheeks like those of its Black-Crested cousin. The fur on the rest of its body is many different shades of gray, which gives it an eerie appearance.

Gray-Cheeked Mangabeys are very shy animals. They live in groups of four to twelve in the trees of the African rain forest. Females only bear one young at a time. They eat leaves, shoots, fruit, hard seeds, and insects.

Many Mangabeys communicate with each other without making a sound. They use a sign language which consists of blinking their eyelids, opening their mouths and flipping their tongues up and down, and opening and shutting their lips, either quickly or slowly. These signals are often followed by some kind of organized action.

THE DOGUERA BABOON

Size:

  Weight: Approximately 100 pounds (45 kilograms)

Habitat:

  Ethiopia and Kenya

Description:

  Doguera Baboons have long muzzles and long tails which they usually hold in an upside down "U" shape. They have powerful muscles, strong jaws and heavy ridges of bone over the eyes. Their arms and legs are of almost equal length.

Studies of baboons are important because these monkeys have forsaken life in the trees and may help us understand why early man made a similar move.

Baboons are fierce fighters and live in large packs. They are big, tough and hefty. The ruff of hair around their shoulders makes their bodies look even bigger so enemies will be scared and stay at a distance.

Baboons organize into armies and the oldest males become generals. Every member of the army helps defend the troop against lions, jackals, cheetahs, hyenas, and leopards. Leopards are their chief enemy.

Baboons eat grass, insects, fruit and lizards, but some have developed a liking for milk and will kill lambs and calves to get some. Male baboons are very possessive and will bite the neck of a female if she doesn't obey. No female baboon has ever been known to leave her group however, probably because their males make them feel protected.

When a baboon is sick or hurt, its family will care for it. When a young one cries, everybody runs to its aid. When baboons are born, everyone gathers around to adore the baby. Baboons love babies so much they have been known to kidnap human babies from native villages.

THE HAMADRYAS BABOON

Size:

Weight: Adult males average 60 pounds (27 kilograms).
Females weigh about 25 pounds (11 kilograms).

Habitat:

Northeastern Africa

Description:

The Hamadryas Baboon has a dog-like face, deeply set eyes,
a long squared muzzle and vicious-looking teeth. The cape
of hair that extends from its shoulders gives it a royal look.

Several ancient cultures considered this baboon sacred.
However, the Egyptians paid it the highest respect. The oldest
known statue from the culture of the Nile is an alabaster figure of
a baboon carved 3400 years before the birth of Christ.

Egyptians favored Hamadryas Baboons probably because of
their habit of sitting solemnly with their hands on their knees,
never looking directly at anyone. Perhaps they resembled the
aloof Egyptian high priests.

These priests tested Baboons to see if they were intelligent. If a
baboon tested well it was judged sacred and given tasks to
perform in the temple. These temple Baboons were given special
privileges and food and some were mummified and buried with
the pharaohs. Baboons who failed the tests became slaves and
were trained to do an amazing variety of jobs in the houses and
fields.

For over three thousand years the Hamadryas Baboon was the
most important animal in Egyptian religious life and art. It was
probably more a part of man's life during that time than any other
animal has been before or since, including the dog.

THE BARBARY APE

Size:

Height: 2 feet (61 centimeters)
Weight: 10-20 pounds (4.5-9 kilograms)

Habitat:

Rock of Gibraltar

Description:

The Barbary Ape is a strong animal with powerful jaws and
a thick, rough, greenish-brown coat. Babies of this species
are almost hairless at birth.

Gibraltar is a large rock island in the Mediterranean Sea which
lies between Spain and Africa. The Barbary Apes who live on this
rock are the only Primates found today in Europe.

No one knows how these animals first got to Gibraltar. They
live in caves high in the rocks and people once believed these
caves went deep into the ground, making a tunnel under the sea to
Africa. There are a few Barbary Apes in the rocky mountain
forests of Northern Africa. However, scientists now believe the
animals on the island were brought there by ship.

The Rock of Gibraltar is owned by Great Britain. The English
have long believed that when the last of the Barbary Apes dies or
leaves Gibraltar the British will disappear too. Because of this
legend, special soldiers guard the Barbary Apes. But the monkeys
sometimes come into town and cause trouble. They steal food and
anything else that interests them. They have terrorized cats, dogs
and chickens and have jumped on people's heads, stealing their
hats, handkerchiefs and even their wigs!

A large male once caused so much trouble he was arrested.
These monkeys are hard to catch, though, because they post
sentries and have very good eyesight.

THE LION-TAILED MACAQUE

<u>Size:</u>
   Weight: Males weigh 14-15 pounds (6.75 kilograms).
<u>Habitat:</u>
   The grasslands and dry areas of scrub and cactus on the southwestern coast of India.
<u>Description:</u>
   The Lion-Tailed Macaque has extremely thick brown or black fur. Its face is framed by a light-colored, wild and bushy mane. And its tail has a lion-like tuft at the end.

Lion-Tailed Macaques are large, imposing animals. They are very shy, but also very fierce. They will threaten anyone who disturbs their forest home. Their dispositions are dangerous, and they have been reported to have killed native children.

Macaques are vicious in captivity if caught and caged as adults. But if taken while young, and not exposed to other monkeys, they will grow into gentle pets.

The Lion-Tails eat fruit, roots, insects, rice, maize, potatoes, and sugar cane. Rarely observed in the wild, they are the least well-known of the Macaques.

The Lion-Tailed Macaque is in danger of extinction.

THE JAPANESE MACAQUE

Size:

Weight: Males 24-40 pounds (11.1-18 kilograms). Females
18-36 pounds (8.3-16.3 kilograms).
Habitat:

Forests of the Japanese islands
Description:

The Japanese Macaque is covered with long, shaggy fur and
has cheek pouches for storing food. During mating season
the faces of both males and females become bright red.

Japanese Macaques are very shy and it's hard to catch a glimpse
of one even in the wild. However, a group of Japanese scientists
was able to lure a troop of these monkeys to an open space where
they could be studied more closely. Many things were learned.

Japanese Macaques communicate by making thirty different
sounds. The scientists were able to record and learn the meaning
of each of these sounds and to reproduce them and receive
answering calls from Macaques in the jungle.

The scientists discovered that Macaques were afraid of the
ocean. To see if they would overcome this fear, the researchers
threw peanuts into the water. The younger monkeys jumped right
in to get them and soon began walking into the sea during the day
to cool off. The older monkeys did not learn to swim but the
young did, and they and their infants soon began swimming and
diving for seaweed out of pure pleasure. And since they are not
afraid of the sea anymore, it has become a playground for all
future generations.

THE CELEBES BLACK APE

Size:

Weight: Males are 23-24 pounds (10.4-11.2 kilograms).
Females are 11-17 pounds (5.1-7.7 kilograms).

Habitat:

The northern peninsula of Celebes, one of the Indonesian
Islands

Description:

The Celebes Ape is jet black, with a long face, a backward-
drooping crest of hair on its head, and pink pads on its rump.

The Celebes Ape is really not an ape at all. A true ape has no
tail, and this monkey has one. But it is so small that it doesn't show.

Celebes Apes stand and walk on all fours like baboons, for
whom they are often mistaken. They have the same head crests
and bony ridges above their eyes.

Coastal tribes in the north of Celebes worship this monkey.
They believe the black apes are their ancestors. To honor them,
they set rafts of food adrift on the river as an offering to the ape
gods.

The Apes are strong animals, but of a quiet and peaceful nature.
They live in harmony with their human island neighbors. It is
believed they first came to Celebes from the Phillipines. But
because there is no animal on the Phillipine Islands resembling
them, their origin remains a mystery.

KIRK'S RED COLOBUS

<u>Size:</u>

   Height: 3½-5 feet (107-152 centimeters)

<u>Habitat:</u>

   The island of Zanzibar, off the east coast of Africa

<u>Description:</u>

   Kirk's Red Colobus has a black body with chestnut brown head, arms and legs. This color combination serves as camouflage. It is a slow moving animal with short forelimbs (arms) and only four fingers on each hand.

    These monkeys live only one place on earth—the island of Zanzibar. And there are only two hundred of them left. They have been hunted for their skins which have been used to make women's coats and hats and shot by farmers trying to protect their crops.

    The Colobus has no thumbs, which account for its name. Colobus is a Greek work meaning "mutilated". People have tried to breed the Colobus in other parts of the world but have failed. These monkeys die when forced to leave Zanzibar.

Kirk's Red Colobus is in danger of extinction.

THE BLACK AND WHITE COLOBUS

Size:

Height: 30-40 inches (76-102 centimeters) with a 2-5 foot (61-152 centimeter) tail

Habitat:

Northeastern Africa

Description:

The Black and White Colobus has a flat, dark, hairless face surrounded by pure white fur. The rest of its coat is jet black with white plumes, a white bushy tail and a long cape of fur. Its nose is hooked and its buttocks bare.

The Black and White Colobus was well known in ancient times, probably even to the Romans. These large monkeys have thick fur that makes them look larger than they really are. When they sit in trees their black capes hang down like jungle moss, and serve as camouflage.

The Colobus is fast and agile and a fine jumper. A leaf-eater, it has a series of stomachs, like a cud-chewing cow. It also eats insects.

In the past, these monkeys were hunted for their skins, highly prized for their thick fur and distinctive markings. They have been used for tribal headdresses and women's coats.

THE DEBRAZZA GUENON

Habitat:
   Rain forests in the Congo

Description:
   The forehead under the black cap of fur on the DeBrazza Guenon's head is pale brown and white. Its pouched cheeks are blue and its upper lip, throat and chin whiskers are white. There is an orange crescent on its forehead and its hands and arms are black.

The DeBrazzas are perhaps the showiest of all the Guenons. They always look handsomely dressed in stunning color.

At home in tall dense forests or small scattered trees, these monkeys spend a lot of time on the ground hunting crickets and grasshoppers, their favorite food. They gallop along like dogs, holding their long tails high in the air.

The colorful DeBrazza baby sucks its thumb, just as a human baby does.

THE DOUC LANGUR

Size:
   Height: 2 feet (61 centimeters)
Habitat:
   Vietnam and Laos
Description:
   One species of Douc Langur has a yellow face and the other
   a black face. This monkey has beautiful slanted eyes and
   thick glossy fur. Long white hair grows from its cheeks and
   there's a red and black band on its forehead. Its body is
   black and maroon, with black palms and feet, white
   forearms and red lower legs. There's a white strip across its
   rump and a completely white tail.

This fantastic animal is one of the most colorful of the Primates.
Its light-colored face and gorgeous dark, slanted eyes give it an
oriental appearance.

Not much is known about these animals. They are thought to
live in large groups in the tropical rain forests.

Douc, pronounced duke, means monkey in Vietnamese. The
war in Vietnam was hard on the doucs. Soldiers, living off the
land, killed many of them. Then bombs and high explosives
destroyed their homes.

The Douc Langur is in danger of extinction.

THE PROBOSCIS LANGUR

Size:
  Height: Males are 2½ feet (76 centimeters) from head to tail
  Weight: 45-50 pounds (20-23 kilograms).
Habitat:
  Forests on the island of Borneo
Description:
  The body of The Proboscis Langur is rust-red, changing to buff at the bottom. Its face is pinkish with small eyes and a huge flesh-colored nose.

The Proboscis is one of the most bizarre monkeys. Adult males look like monkey Pinocchios with noses sometimes four inches long. An old male's nose will sometimes hang down below his chin. It is believed that the females liked the males with the largest noses best and always picked them as mates. So the babies' noses kept getting longer and longer.

Surprisingly, their noses don't get in the way when they eat. These monkeys are leaf eaters but also eat palm shoots and fruit. They are often found lying on their backs sunning themselves and don't like to be disturbed when in this relaxed state. The young love to playfully tease their parents by tweaking their noses or swinging on their tails.

Proboscis are usually very calm animals but they make a lot of noise when traveling through the treetops. Swimming is their favorite thing. On hot days they like to drop into a stream and do the dogpaddle.

THE CELANESE GRAY LANGUR

<u>Size:</u>
Height: 2 feet (161 centimeters) long with tail 2½ feet (176 centimeters) long
Weight: Males weigh 20-30 pounds (9.0 kilograms). Females weigh 6-15 pounds (4.3 kilograms).

<u>Habitat:</u>
India and Ceylon

<u>Description:</u>
There are twenty different kinds of Langur Monkeys. Some have purple faces, some are golden all over. Many are very colorful. The Celanese Gray Langur's face is black and its gray fur is rippled with buff and silver. The Grey Langur is a slender, beautiful monkey.

The baby Langur must feel very loved. Its mother and aunts and other female monkeys take turns passing it around, hugging and licking it. Mothers are proud of their babies but will not share their food with them. The little ones must find their own. Father Langurs don't come near their children. They will not even protect them from danger.

In India Hanuman Langur monkeys are sacred. No one may harm a Langur. Foreigners have been killed for interfering with them. They are free to roam the streets and even though these monkeys steal from the temples they are allowed to stay there. Storeowners put iron bars on their shops so the monkeys won't steal from them. Priests feed these monkeys regularly and give grain to them even though human babies in India are starving.

THE MANDRILL

Size:

Height: 33 inches (84 centimeters) long with stumpy 5-inch (10 centimeter) tail

Habitat:

Western Central Africa: Cameroon, Rio Muni, Gabon and the Congo

Description:

Mandrills have large bodies with thick, straight black hair. Their snouts are doglike with rows of yellowish teeth, some of which are four inches long. They have bright blue cheeks, red noses and white whiskers. Their beards and the ruff of fur which extends around their shoulders are orange. Their buttocks are purple and scarlet.

Mandrills, or forest baboons, are strong, heavy, compact monkeys with tremendous muscles. Their bodies slope backwards when they stand on all fours and they walk on their fingers and toes, palms never touching the ground. Mandrills are as strong as leopards and as powerful as gorillas when enraged. When a Mandrill is angry the colors on its face get even brighter because of the increased blood circulation.

These monkeys spend most of their day looking under rocks for ants and insects, but they will eat anything. They can locate water by digging in dry riverbeds. Although they are ferocious looking beasts Mandrills are very cautious and have formed friendly relationships with people while in captivity.

The Mandrill will probably become an endangered species within the next few years because West African natives hunt them for food. They like Mandrill meat better than any other.

The Apes

THE APES

Most of the experts today agree that the mammals we call Apes evolved from monkeys some fifty million years ago. With the exception of man, they are the most advanced form of Primates. Apes differ from monkeys because they are much larger and they have no tails.

There are two categories of apes, the Lesser Apes and the Great Apes. The Lesser Apes are called Gibbons and are found mostly in the Orient and down through Malaya and Java and Borneo. Siamangs are intermediate apes and live in Malaya and Sumatra.

There are three kinds of Great Apes—Chimpanzees, Orangutans, and Gorillas. Orangutans are found in Borneo while Chimpanzees and Gorillas make Africa their home.

THE LAR GIBBON

Size:

Height: 3 feet (91 centimeters) tall

Habitat:

Indonesia, Indochina, Thailand, and Burma

Description:

Six species of Gibbon exist. The males of some species are black, females are light brown. Both sexes are white when born and gradually change color as they grow.

Gibbons are great acrobats. They love to swing through the trees and go so fast it sometimes looks like they are flying. They walk vines like high wire artists, something no other monkey is able to do. Gibbons can catch birds in mid-air as they swing from branch to branch. They don't have many enemies because they're so fast no one can catch them.

Gibbons are slender with beautiful soft fur. Their arms are one and a half times longer than their legs and they have no tail. On the ground they walk on two legs most of the time, like people.

Perhaps because of this trait and their loud, mournful calls, a strange belief has arisen in Burma. There the people think Gibbons are disappointed lovers who have been reincarnated. Some natives will not kill them because they believe they are human.

THE SIAMANG

Size:
   Weight: 40 pounds (18 kilograms)
Habitat:
   Malaysia and Indonesia
Description:
   Siamangs are entirely black with shaggy fur and hairless
   faces. The red vocal sacs in their throats inflate to the size of
   their heads when they give their call.

Siamangs live in pairs and can leap forty-five feet between
trees. They are surly animals and get vicious as they get older.
Each day when the sun rises and sets they make a tremendous
noise. They also use their powerful voices to warn neighbors of
danger. Because of their throat sacs they can make more noise
than almost any other living animal except the Howler.

Although they often race along tree limbs like madmen, waving
their great arms and howling and roaring, the Gibbons were
always thought by the Chinese to be the aristocrat of the monkey
kingdom.

THE ORANGUTAN

Size:

Height: Males are approximately 4½ feet (137 centimeters). Females are about 3½ feet (117 centimeters).

Weight: Males weigh about 250 pounds (113 kilograms). Females weigh half as much.

Habitat:

The island of Borneo

Description:

The Orangutan is grotesque looking with huge protruding cheeks and large flaps on the neck formed by the voice sacs. Their dark gray skin is coarse and sparsely covered with reddish hair. Young Orangutans have blue-tinted faces. These are huge animals. Some adults have an armspread of eight feet.

The Orangutan, or "Old Man of the Woods" as it is sometimes called, grows up in the trees. But as they get older these huge beasts get too heavy for the branches and have to live on ground. They roam the forests, and make a new nest to sleep in every night.

Like the Howler and the Siamang, Orangutans have large vocal sacs and can make a tremendous roar. They also use these sacs to make loud burping noises to scare away intruders. They sometimes also hurl sticks.

There are not many of these apes left in the world. They are disappearing for several reasons. Since human headhunting is against the law, some tribes now hunt Orangutans instead. Their forests are being cut away to make farmland, and hunters are catching many of them and sending them to zoos.

The Orangutan is in danger of extinction.

THE CHIMPANZEE

Size:

    Height: 3-5 feet (91-152 centimeters)
    Weight: About 150 pounds (68 kilograms)

Habitat:

    African tropical rain forests from the Niger basin to Angola

Description:

    The Chimpanzee's face is black and hairless. Its ears, hands, and feet are also furless but flesh-colored. Long black hair covers the rest of its body except for a white patch on the rump. Chimps normally walk on all fours but they can walk upright.

Chimpanzees prefer fruit to any other food. A large boy chimpanzee can eat over fifty bananas at one time. Chimps spend most of their time in trees and love to make noise. They also like attention and affection. When a Chimp returns from hunting with food its friends will gather around and hug and kiss it. Chimps sometimes even bow to one another and hold hands. If a Chimp is hurt the other will nurse it back to health.

Chimps hate rain but instead of finding shelter they do wild rain dances. However, they are very intelligent animals, and have even learned to make and use primitive tools.

THE MOUNTAIN GORILLA

Size:

    Height: Males are about 5 feet 8 inches (173 centimeters).
    Females are approximately 4 feet 8 inches (142 centimeters).
    Weight: 450-600 pounds (204-272 kilograms).

Description:

    Mountain Gorillas are distinguished from Lowland and Western Gorillas by shorter arms, long silky hair and strikingly man-like feet. The male has a crest on the top of his head which gives a helmet-like effect. Gorillas normally walk on all fours with knuckles to the ground.

The gorilla is the largest ape. It has dark hair, black skin and grows as tall as a man. The leopard and natives of tribes who eat gorilla meat are its only enemies.

Gorillas live in small families and don't fight with each other. They like to relax and lie in the sun when not looking for food. When male Gorillas are ten years old they grow silver hairs on their backs and one becomes leader of the group. Silverback males will glare at young gorillas or slap the ground if they get too noisy or play too rough. When females start screaming at each other the leader glares at them and they calm down. And when a silverback male pulls a leaf from a plant and puts it between his lips, watch out! It is a signal he is going to get violent. But the leader is usually gentle with his family. Females nestle against him and babies crawl all over his huge body.

Gorillas do not eat other animals—only plants. They are afraid of water and don't even like to cross small streams. They like to build nests—in the trees and on the ground. Sometimes a gorilla will build a nest on a hillside and roll out and down the hill during the night in his sleep.

Recent experiments have shown that gorillas are very intelligent. One gorilla has shown the remarkable ability to learn over three hundred seventy five signs in sign language and has demonstrated the I.Q. of a young child.

The Mountain Gorilla is in danger of extinction.

BIBLIOGRAPHY

Amon, Aline. *Orangutan Endangered Ape*. New York: Atheneum, 1977.

Annixter, Jane and Paul. *Monkeys and Apes*. New York: Franklin Watts, 1976.

Berrill, Jacqueline. *Wonders of the Monkey World*. New York: Dodd, Mead and Company, 1967.

Bourne, Geoffrey. *The Ape People*. New York: G.P. Putnam's Sons, 1971.

———*Primate Odyssey*. New York: G.P. Putnam's Sons, 1974.

Burton, Dr. Maurice and Robert, (general editors). *The International Wildlife Encyclopedia*. New York: Marshall Cavendish Corporation, 1969.

Cook, David and Jill Hughes. *A Closer Look at Apes*. New York: Franklin Watts, 1976.

Gardner, Richard. *The Baboon*. New York: The Macmillan Co., 1972.

Groves, Colin P. *Gorillas*. New York: Arco Publishing Company, Inc., 1970.

Hess, Lilo. *Monkeys and Apes Without Trees*. New York: Charles Scribner's Sons, 1973.

Kenles, Bettyann. *Watching The Wild Apes*. New York: E.P. Dutton and Co., Inc.,1976.

Lemmon, Robert S. *All About Monkeys*. New York: Random House, 1958.

MacKinnon. *In Search of the Red Ape*. New York: Holt, Rinehart and Winston, 1974.

———*The Ape Within Us*. New York: Holt, Rinehart and Winston, 1978.

Napier, John Russell. *A Handbook of Living Primates*. New York: Academic Press, 1967.

———*The Roots of Mankind*. Washington, D.C.: Smithsonian Institution Press, 1970.

Napier, Prue. *Monkeys and Apes*. New York: Grosset & Dunlap, 1972. .

Reynolds, Vernon. *The Apes*. New York: E.P. Dutton and Co., Inc., 1967.

Rosen, Stephen I. *Introduction to the Primates*. New Jersey: Prentice-Hall, 1974.

Sanderson, Ivan T. *The Monkey Kingdom*. New York: Doubleday and Co., Inc., 1957.

Schultz. *The Life of Primates*. Great Britain: Weidenfeld and Nicolson, 1969.

Snell, Roy J. *Monkeyland*. Chicago: The Reilly and Lee Company, 1941.

VanLawick-Goodall, Baroness Jane. *My Friends the Wild Chimpanzees*. Washington, D.C.: The National Geographic Society, 1967.

Walker, Ernest P. *The Monkey Book*. New York: The MacMillan Company, 1954.

Yerkes, Robert M. *Almost Human*. New York: The Century Company, 1925.

INDEX

acrobats 82

alabaster 55

albino 21

ancient 55

ape gods. 63

apes 9, 63, 81, 91

aristocrats. 85

armspread 87

bizarre. 73

burping 87

bush bear 17

callous 43

camouflage 67

Capuchin Monks 29

cavalrymen 47

cheek pouches 49

chest rubbers. 39

crescent. 68

crowned eagle 45

decoy 47

dinosaurs 9

dogpaddle 73

equator 43

extinction 9

ferocious. 77

"fifth hand" 25

forest baboons 77

fossils. 13

ghastly. 32

ghostly 21

Great Apes.................................81
grimacers 49
grotesque 87
half monkey 13
head crests................................63
headdresses 67
headhunting................................87
honey bear.................................17
hood 27
hysterical 32
leaf eaters 67
Lesser Apes 81
mammals 9, 81
military monkeys 47
monkey Pinocchios 73
muscular pads..............................15
mushrooms..................................47
mutilated 65
New World 25
Nile 55
Old Man of the Woods 87
Old World 43
organ grinders.............................29
owl..45
packs 53
pharaohs...................................55
plumes 67
pre-monkeys 9, 13
priests 55
Primates 9
"Primate Cheetahs" 47

primitive 89
Prosimian 13
poison 32
rain dances 89
reincarnated 19, 82
reptiles 9
sacred baboon 55
sacred langurs 75
saliva 39
signals 57
Silverback 91
slaves 55
species 9
spines 17
sobbing 39
"softly, softly" 17
somersaults 32
sound boxes 31
spooky 15
sun worshippers 19
toilet trained 39
terrier 31
train 31
tree bear 17
tropical 43
tunnel 57
twins 34
vocal sacs 85, 87
watchdog 47

The number of books that may be
drawn at one time by the card holder is
governed by the reasonable needs of
the reader and the material on hand.
　　Books for junior readers are subject
to special rules.